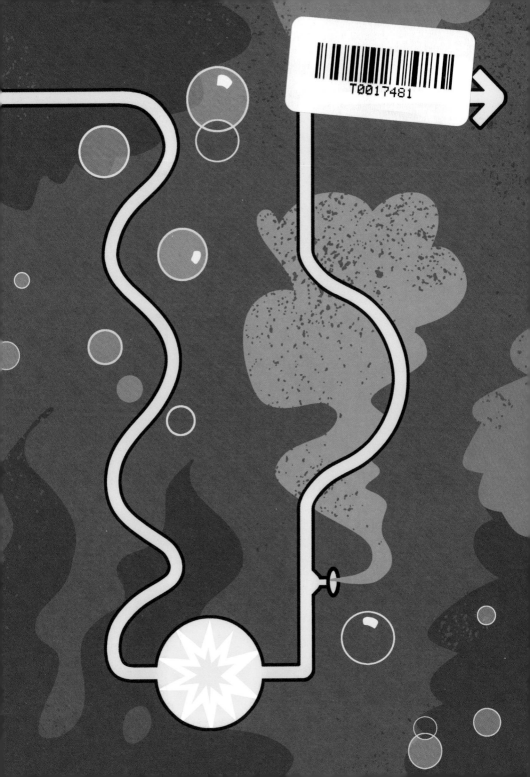

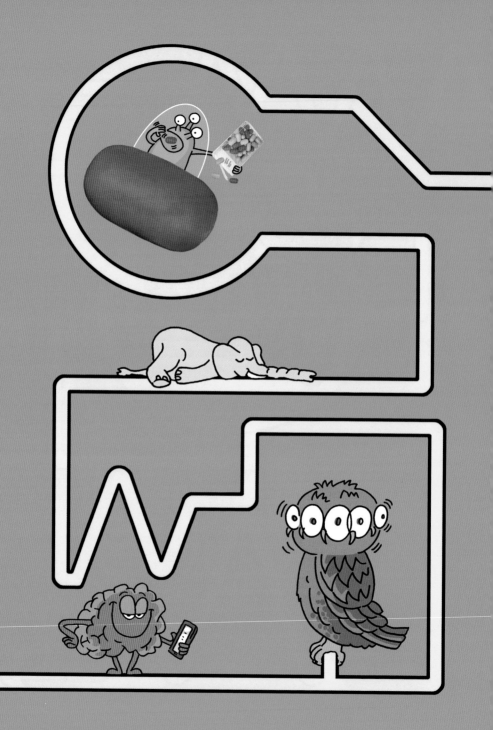

SCIENCE

FACTopia!

STEM-tastic

Follow the TRAIL of 400 FACTS

By ROSE DAVIDSON

Illustrated by ANDY SMITH

BRITANNICA BOOKS

CONTENTS

Welcome back to FACTopia!

Put on your lab coat and get ready to set off on another adventure through hundreds of mind-blowing, wow-worthy, and crazily cool facts all about science. For example...

Did you know that to test if an object is a fossil or just a rock, scientists sometimes lick it?

Scientists do some wacky experiments! They've even performed tests on astronaut poop.

Speaking of space, seeds once sent on a mission to the moon were planted on Earth and grew into "moon trees."

Watch out for trees... the seeds from a sandbox tree can explode, launching them through the forest at 160 miles an hour (258km/h)!

Super speed! The fastest species of ant could run at up to 400 miles an hour (644 km/h) if it were as big as a human.

You might have spotted that there is something special about being here in FACTopia. Every fact is *linked to the next*, and in the most surprising and even hilarious ways.

On this tour of the wonderful world of science, you will encounter **jaw-dropping discoveries, wild weather, cool tools, wacky professions,** and... well, you'll see. Discover what each turn of the page will bring!

But there isn't just one trail through this book. Your path branches every now and then, and you can go to a totally different (but still connected) part of the book by **flipping backward** or **zooming forward.** →⌐

Let your curiosity take you wherever it leads. Of course, a good place to start could be right here, at the beginning.........

For example, take this detour to

find out about gadgets and gizmos

Go to page 152

At 12 years old, England's Mary Anning was the first person to discover a fossil from the ancient marine reptile *Ichthyosaurus*, which means "**fish lizard**"

Scientists discovered **an ancient species of parrot** as tall as a three-year-old and nicknamed it **"SQUAWKZILLA"**

Go to page 14 ↑

More music, please!

Lucy, the **famous skeleton** of an early human ancestor who lived about 3.2 million years ago, was named after a song by The Beatles, an English rock band......

When a paleontologist is unsure if an object is a rock or a fossil, they sometimes **test it with a lick**: If their tongue sticks to it, it's a fossil; if it doesn't, then it's just a rock...

Time to experiment →

In a study to **test pigs' smarts**, scientists trained the pigs to play video games. The result: They learned to use a joystick

Go to page 148

Get more games

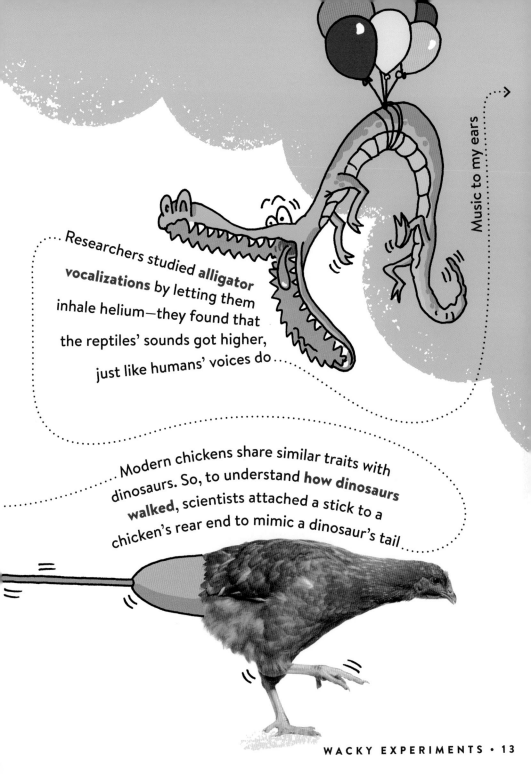

Music to my ears

Researchers studied **alligator vocalizations** by letting them inhale helium—they found that the reptiles' sounds got higher, just like humans' voices do ...

Modern chickens share similar traits with dinosaurs. So, to understand **how dinosaurs walked**, scientists attached a stick to a chicken's rear end to mimic a dinosaur's tail

Scientists found that when music is

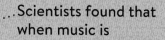

PLAYED
FOR
SOME
PLANTS

those plants will grow faster than plants left in silence.........

There are over **400,000 species of plants**, at least half of which are edible, but humans eat only about 200 of them...

...Moss can absorb 20 times its weight in water, so people have used it to **make diapers**...

Go to page 158

Light it up!

Oak trees are **struck by lightning** more than any other type of tree—this is because they're usually taller than surrounding trees and contain a lot of water, which helps conduct electricity through their trunks.

Some **plants have teeth**! To ward off predators, the rock nettle grows superstrong needlelike hairs containing calcium phosphate—the same element that makes up bones and teeth...

Corpse flowers— plants that produce a **giant, rotten-smelling flower**—can heat themselves to over 90 degrees Fahrenheit (32°C), which helps attract pollinating flies and beetles...

Chomp on these

PLANTS • 17

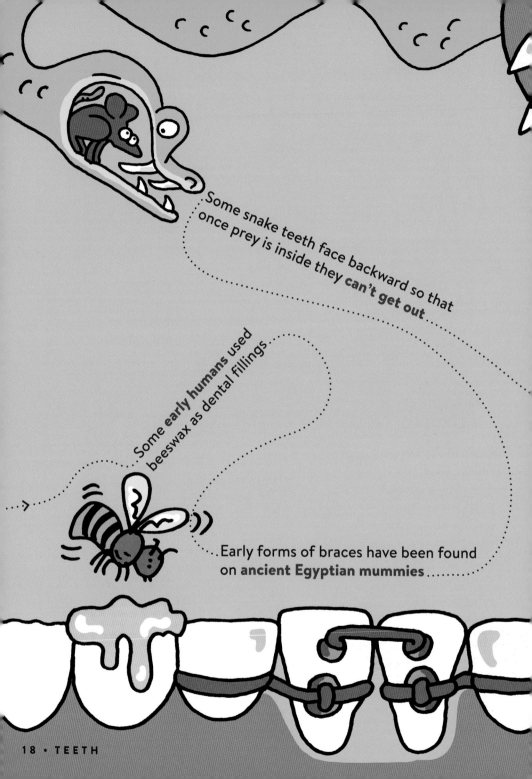

Some snake teeth face backward so that once prey is inside they **can't get out**

Some **early humans** used beeswax as dental fillings

Early forms of braces have been found on **ancient Egyptian mummies**

...Sharks' teeth are in rows, so that when a shark **loses a tooth**, a replacement just moves forward like it's on a conveyor belt...

Keep moving

......Naked mole rats have two bottom teeth that can **move on their own**, like knitting needles.....

The taller you are, the faster you'll go on a swing.

Sloths are one of the slowest mammals on land, but they can move up

There's a company creating

ROBOTIC BOOTS

that, while you're wearing virtual reality gear, will make you feel like you're walking around—even though you're not moving anywhere...

Into another reality....

to three times faster when swimming....

One of the first virtual-reality experiences was created in the late 1950s. Called the Sensorama, it simulated a **motorcycle ride** through a city—even allowing viewers to smell the motor's exhaust.................

Some doctors use virtual reality to **train for surgery**.....

Virtual-reality technology **tricks your brain** into thinking you're looking at the real world, not a screen. It does this by projecting a slightly different image into each of your eyes, which mimics the way your real vision works.........

Instead of live animals, Circus Roncalli in Germany uses **3D images** of elephants, lions, horses, and more...

See some more >

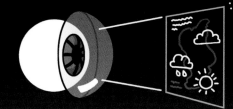

One company is working on using augmented-reality technology to make contact lenses that could **display text messages** and the weather forecast, or even help us see better in low light...

An ostrich's eye is bigger than its **brain**.

By studying the movement of **Saturn**'s rings, **scientists** have discovered that Saturn's core is shaking.

A manta ray's **brain** has a special network of **blood vessels** that surrounds it. This helps to keep the brain warm so the manta ray can dive down into cold water for food.

Scientists have seen **auroras** on other planets, such as Jupiter and **Saturn**.

Your **blood vessels** are likely the reason behind **ice-cream** headaches—the blood vessels in your mouth quickly go from smaller to larger when you eat something cold. Your brain interprets this quick change as pain.

Some types of **ice cream** include an ingredient called a stabilizer that's made from **seaweed**. It helps to stop your treat from melting too fast!

A group of scientists published a paper that argued octopuses are aliens from outer space.

The size of small olives, the eggs of one species of deep-sea octopus can take four and a half years to hatch! That's longer than any other known animal.

Oxygen is responsible for the green and deep red colors of auroras.

Seaweed and microscopic marine algae are responsible for creating more than half the oxygen we breathe.

Take your time

Go to page 16

Blooming botany

Botanists in 19th-century Sweden created clock-shaped gardens that could tell time: At every hour between 3 a.m. and 8 p.m., a different flower would bloom

More than 1,000 years ago, the people of the Song Dynasty in China used **clocks with incense inside.** They could tell the time based on the clocks' smell, which changed as the layers of incense burned.

An astronomical clock shows not only the time, but also the current positions of the sun, moon, Earth, and constellations relative to one another.

Out of this world!

In 1835, a newspaper printed a fictional story about an astronomer who discovered beaches, pyramids, and animals—such as small zebras and beavers walking upright—on the moon. The story is now known as the "Great Moon Hoax".

S2, a star in the Milky Way, travels around a **supermassive black hole** in a flower-shaped orbit ......

...... The four corners of the Great Pyramid of Giza point north, south, east, and west. Ancient Egyptians may have used **astronomy** to position the pyramid in this way......

Go back in time ......>

The **Egyptian hieroglyph** for addition was a pair of legs walking in the direction of the text. The symbol for subtraction was a pair of legs walking away from the text

Using a tool that measures the kinds of light given off by different materials, scientists figured out that a **dagger buried with King Tut** was made from a meteorite

Ancient Egyptians used the length from their elbows to the tip of their middle fingers as a measurement unit called a cubit

Go to page 40

More space rocks

The ancient Egyptians thought the heart was the **center of intelligence**, so it was the only major organ left inside a mummy. The brain was liquefied and removed through the nose........................

Mind blown!

The ancient Egyptians invented their own breath mints to **mask bad breath**

The average person has more than **6,000 THOUGHTS A DAY.**

Scientists think the human brain can store at least a petabyte of information—that's at least **4,000 times** more than a smartphone...

It's making sense

...Your eyes send images to the brain that are

upside down

Your brain, though, interprets the images the

RIGHT WAY UP

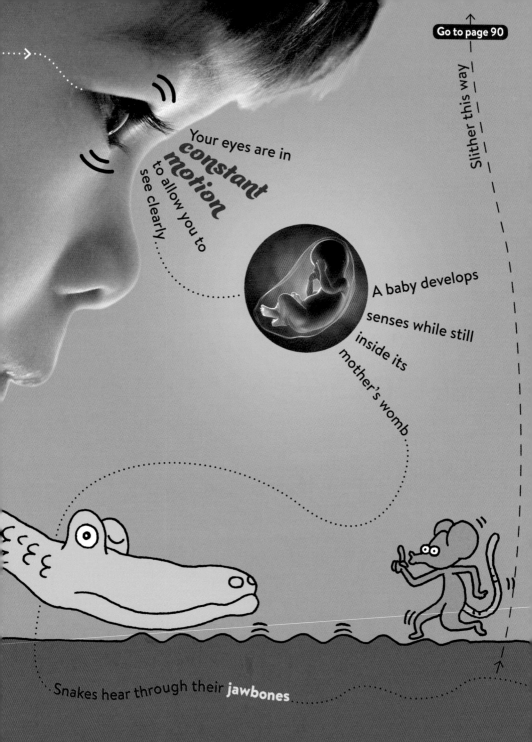

Go to page 90

Slither this way

Your eyes are in **constant motion** to allow you to see clearly

A baby develops senses while still inside its mother's womb

Snakes hear through their **jawbones**

African elephants can use their **sense of smell** to tell the difference between tribes of people.

Gone fishing

Many fish have taste buds on their **fins and tails** as well as in their mouths.

Researchers recently discovered a tiny shark with pockets behind its gills. The pockets contain **glowing goo** that the shark releases to distract and hunt prey in dark water.

Though fish can't talk,
the human voice box
EVOLVED
FROM GILLS.
What did you say?

A teacher from Belfast, Northern Ireland, holds the world record for the loudest shout—it's 121.7 decibels, which is nearly as loud as a jet **engine**.

Some car **engines** can be modified to run using **vegetable** oil that has already been used to make french fries.

Camels have long eyelashes. This special adaptation helps stop desert sand from getting into their **eyes**.

The ancient Romans thought the **giraffe** was a cross between a leopard and a **camel**.

Unlike human eyes, a reindeer's **eyes** can see **ultraviolet light**, which helps them survive the long, dark winter months in the Arctic.

Pigs are protected from harmful rays of **ultraviolet light** because the **mud** they roll in acts as sunscreen.

Mud pots are bubbling pools of mud, caused by **volcanic** activity.

Even though most cooks classify them as **vegetables**, according to botanists **tomatoes** are berries.

Millions of **tomato seeds** that had been in space for six years were brought back to Earth and given to school children to see how they would grow. The space seeds grew just as well as seeds found on Earth—some even produced more fruit.

Acacia **trees** send chemical signals through the air to warn other trees when animals, such as **giraffes**, are eating their leaves. The other acacias respond by pumping toxic chemicals into their leaves, making them taste bitter.

Seeds from the sandbox **tree** can explode through the forest at speeds of up to 160 miles an hour (258km/h).

Millions of **diamond** particles can be found in the **flame** of a candle.

Gas, dust, and rocks make up comets, which are also known as "dirty snowballs."

A kimberlite eruption is a type of **volcanic** eruption that brings up materials that form **diamonds**.

The **flame** produced by burning methane **gas** is blue.

That rocks!

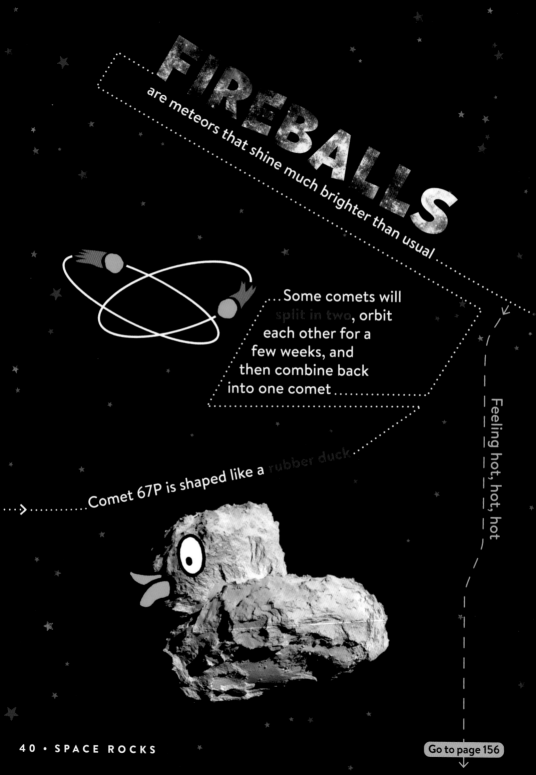

FIREBALLS

are meteors that shine much brighter than usual

Some comets will split in two, orbit each other for a few weeks, and then combine back into one comet

Comet 67P is shaped like a rubber duck

Feeling hot, hot, hot

Go to page 156

About 150 asteroids in our solar system have their own moons.

An asteroid between Mars and Jupiter called 16 Psyche contains gold and other precious metals that could be worth up to **$10,000 quadrillion.**

Dig for gold ......>

There is a little bit of gold in **every person's blood.**

About the body

Eucalyptus roots can **transfer gold** from the ground into the tree's leaves

Go to page 144

Good genes

There is a gene that determines whether your **earwax is wet or dry.**

The **human bladder** can hold up to two cups (473ml) of pee.

You're **taller in the morning** than you are at night, because during the day the water-filled disks that sit between the bones of your spine get compressed by Earth's gravity.

The average human has about **10,000 taste buds**. Old taste buds are replaced with new taste buds about every two weeks.

There are up to 100,000 miles (160,934km) of **blood vessels** in the human body.

Go with the blood flow..........7

The U.S. president's limo has a fridge stocked with the **president's blood type** in case of an emergency.

Horseshoe crabs have **bright blue blood** that has antibacterial properties. Scientists use it to test new vaccines for harmful bacteria.

Medical marvels

Go to page 164

Butterflies will drink **spilled blood** for extra nutrients

Eat up ··· ⟩

The pumpkin's ancestor was a **squash the size of a tennis ball** that used to be eaten by mastodons..........

Research shows that the best nutrient-dense **food of the future** will include algae, kelp, fungi protein, and insects.....

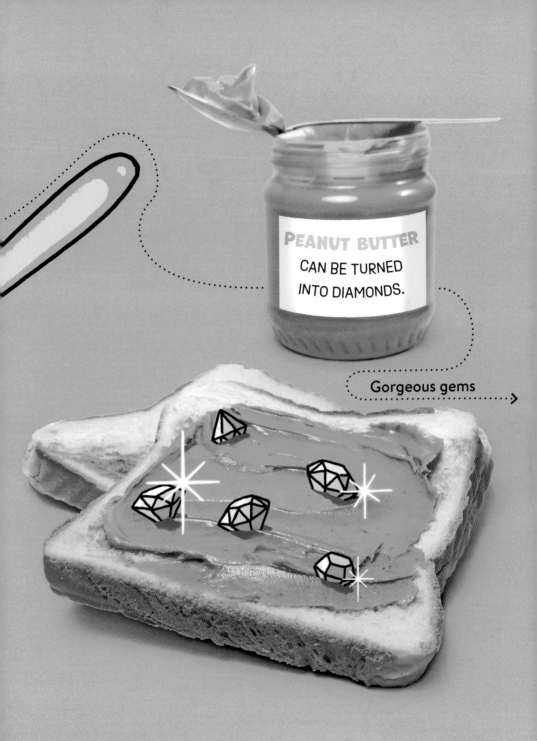

PEANUT BUTTER

CAN BE TURNED

INTO DIAMONDS.

Gorgeous gems ⟶

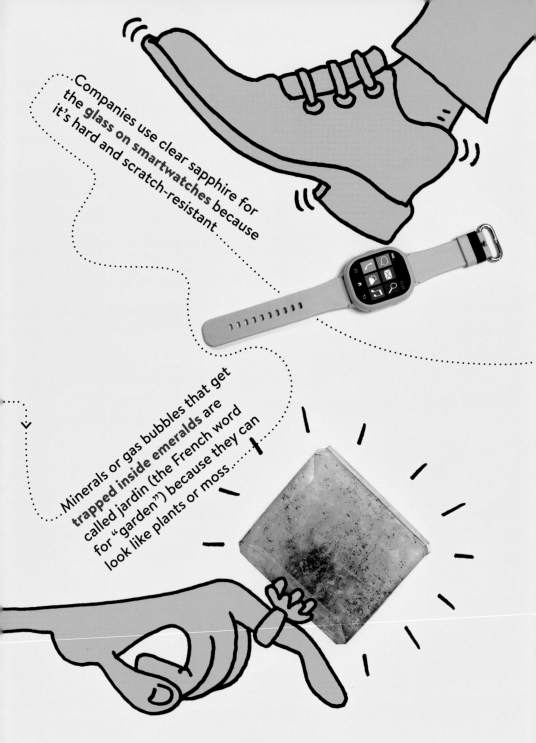

Companies use clear sapphire for the **glass on smartwatches** because it's hard and scratch-resistant

Minerals or gas bubbles that get **trapped inside emeralds** are called jardin (the French word for "garden") because they can look like plants or moss

There are ants that "mine" garnets: They move these gemstones, called **anthill garnets**, to the surface while they dig tunnels.

If the world's **fastest species of ant** were the size of a person, it could run up to 400 miles an hour (644km/h).

Speed into sports

Recent studies show that when **tennis players grunt** as they hit the ball, it is more difficult for their opponent to predict its direction.

Both Olympic athletes and experts at other types of games, such as chess grandmasters, have **longer life spans** than the average human.

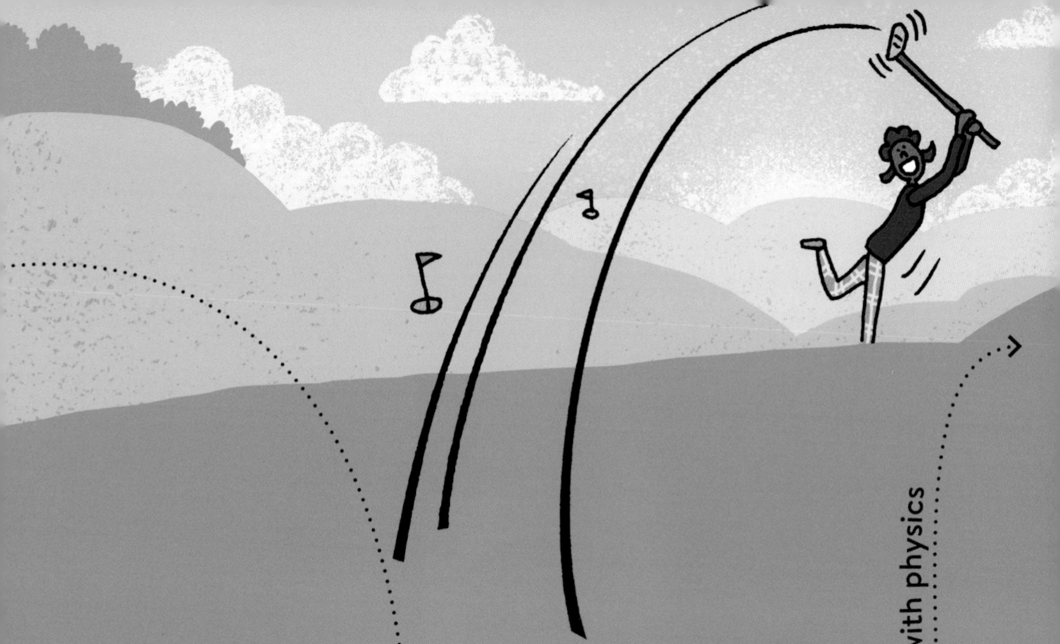

Fun with physics

If a golf ball didn't have

DIMPLES,

it would travel only half the distance. The dimples allow air to flow in a way that minimizes the drag, or the force acting against the ball, letting it travel farther.

If you dropped a feather and a bowling ball at the same time on the moon, they would hit the ground simultaneously. On Earth, the resistance from air makes the feather fall more slowly.

Go to page 132

More on the moon

Researchers at CERN, the particle physics laboratory in Switzerland, are trying to replicate the

BIG BANG,

the event that created the universe.

Grab your goggles →

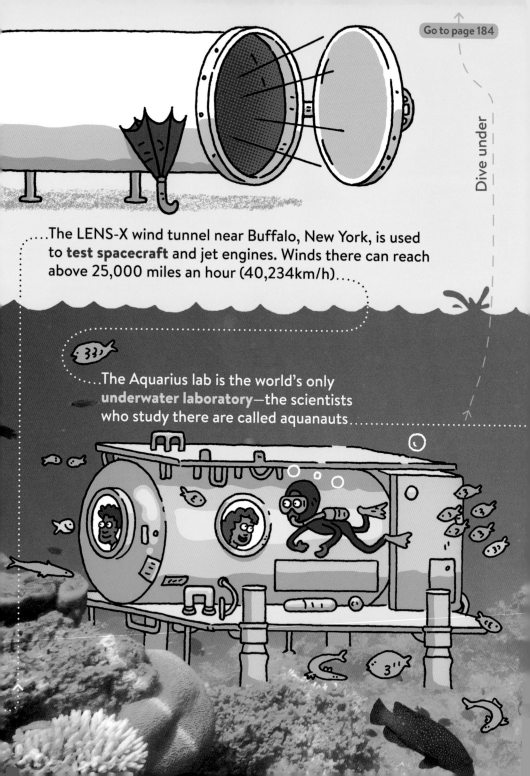

Go to page 184

Dive under

The LENS-X wind tunnel near Buffalo, New York, is used to **test spacecraft** and jet engines. Winds there can reach above 25,000 miles an hour (40,234km/h).

The Aquarius lab is the world's only **underwater laboratory**—the scientists who study there are called aquanauts.

The **highest laboratory** of all time sat at 17,598 feet (5,364m) on Mount Everest.

Poop from astronauts on the **International Space Station** has been brought back to Earth to be studied in labs.

Scientists can **grow diamonds** in a lab.

So sparkly

Testing, testing

Go to page 12

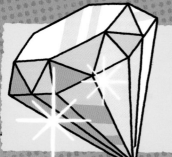

Diamonds are the **hardest** natural substance humans have ever discovered on Earth.

Scientists think the **hardest** material in the universe may be what's called nuclear pasta—a material that makes up part of **neutron stars**, massive stars that have collapsed.

When **neutron stars** crash into each other they can create an explosion called a kilonova, which can produce platinum and **gold**.

Pyrite, commonly called fool's **gold**, is used to make car **batteries**.

You can make **batteries** out of potatoes by putting **metal** nails on both ends. Just one potato could power an LED light bulb for more than a month.

Koalas' bodies allow them to break down the toxic chemical in eucalyptus leaves, making them safe to eat.

Instead of plastic pieces that never decompose, Earth-friendly **glitter** is made from eucalyptus trees—the same trees that **koalas** like to eat from.

Cool chemistry

A **mineral** called mica, considered nature's **glitter**, is used in lipsticks and car paints.

When sand gets **hot** enough to melt, it forms a liquid **mineral** used to make glass. Other minerals can be added to change its color.

The strongest **metal**, tungsten, melts at 6,192 degrees Fahrenheit (3,422°C). That's about 14 times as **hot** as the temperature needed to bake a pizza.

An

is an extremely light solid that is like an almost see-through sponge. Scientists have used aerogels to collect dust from a **comet's tail**

When table salt burns, it makes a

yellow flame

The **hydrogen atoms** in your body are some of the same ones that were present when the universe was created billions of years ago.

Totally elementary

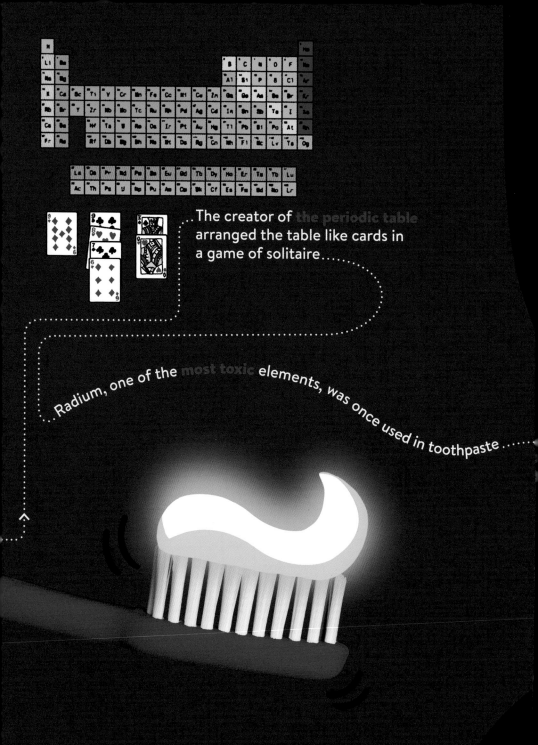

The creator of the periodic table arranged the table like cards in a game of solitaire.

Radium, one of the most toxic elements, was once used in toothpaste

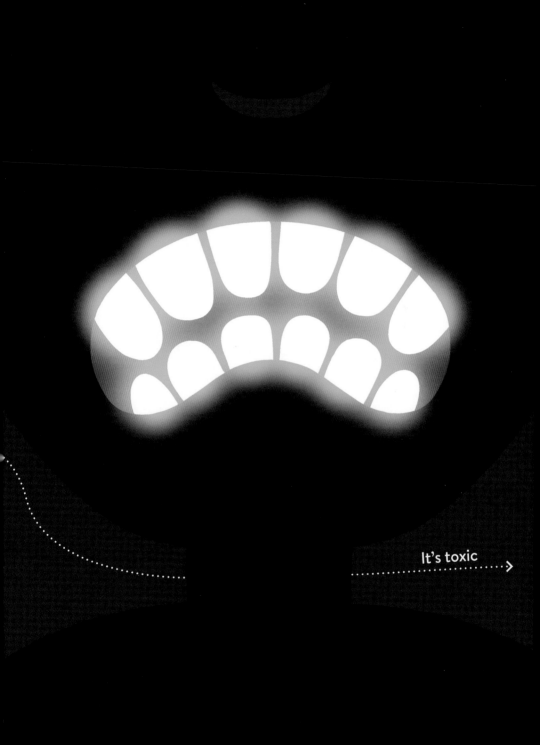

It's toxic ·······>

Cone snails have a **needlelike tooth** that they can shoot at their prey, injecting them with venom.

Howler monkeys sometimes eat **poisonous plants**, but scientists think the clay they also eat counteracts the poison.

Dive in →

In order to defend themselves,
sea slugs **steal venom** from jellyfish
by eating the jelly's tentacles

Marine scientists think there are more human artifacts that have sunk in the ocean than exist in all the world's museums.

Only **one-fifth of the ocean floor** has been mapped by scientists

There are **lakes and rivers** on the seafloor—some even have their own waves

Don't blow it >

Underwater volcanoes can form bubbles large enough to **swallow a ship.**

Some corals make their own "sunscreen" by producing **bright colors,** which attract algae that help shield the corals from harmful rays ....

A soap bubble created in Poland was big enough to fit 417 people inside.

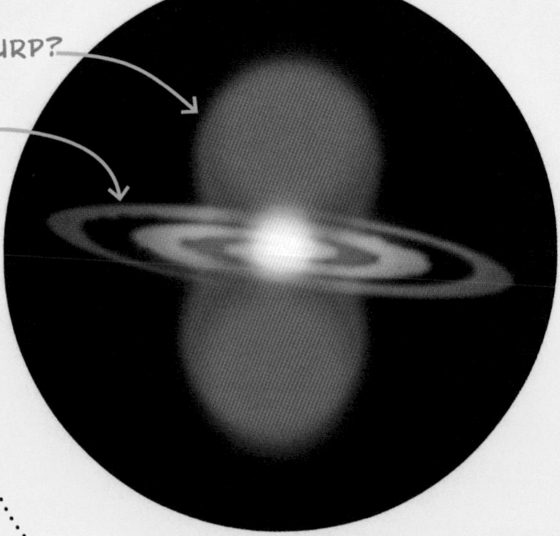

COULD THIS BE A BURP?

MILKY WAY

......There are two giant
gas-filled bubbles
in the Milky Way galaxy.
Researchers think they
might be "burps" from
the star-eating black hole
in the galaxy's center...

Feeling gassy

Some catfish in France's Tarn River have adapted to hunt pigeons. The large **fish** jump out of the water onto land and then drag their **bird** prey back into the water.

Physicists are studying **birds' nests** to learn how strong structures can be built from very light materials.

When disturbed, **ocean-dwelling** sea squirts contract their bodies and squirt water—and sometimes even squirt out their stomachs—to repel **fish** that might eat them.

Ruby-throated hummingbirds build their tiny **nests** with plants and use **spiderwebs** to help hold them together.

The pull of **gravity** from the moon and sun causes the tides in our **oceans**.

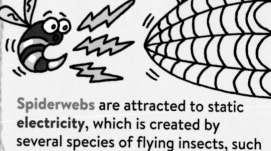

Spiderwebs are attracted to static **electricity**, which is created by several species of flying insects, such as bees, when they fly. This allows the web to bend closer to prey, helping spiders catch their meal.

The gas, dust, and stars in a galaxy are held together by **gravity**.

The tip of the Washington Monument in the U.S. capital is made of solid **aluminum**. The metal was chosen because it would withstand **lightning** strikes.

Heat from a **lightning** strike can cause sap from a **tree** to boil and the water inside the trunk to turn into steam—which can cause a tree to explode.

"Moon **trees**" grew from **seeds** taken to the moon and back on a 1971 space mission.

The exhaust fumes from race **cars** can reach 1,800 degrees Fahrenheit (982°C)—that's hot enough to melt **aluminum**.

Orchids produce the world's smallest **seeds**—each one is the size of a piece of **dust**.

Electricity first started powering early versions of electric **cars** in the early 1800s—nearly 200 years before the first Tesla hit the road.

All of the elements in the human body originally came from space **dust**.

Blast off!

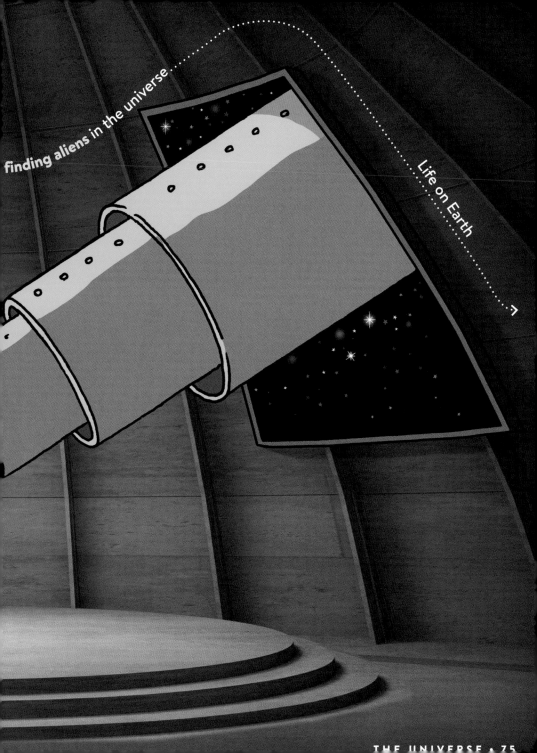

finding aliens in the universe.....

Life on Earth ....

Go to page 10

Dig up more

..In 1868, a paleontologist presenting a **fossil** of the newly discovered marine reptile *Elasmosaurus* accidentally put the skull on the fossil's tail rather than its neck ......

..In 2021, scientists stumbled upon a **nano-chameleon** as small as a sunflower seed! Named *Brookesia nana*, the new chameleon is the tiniest known reptile on Earth ......

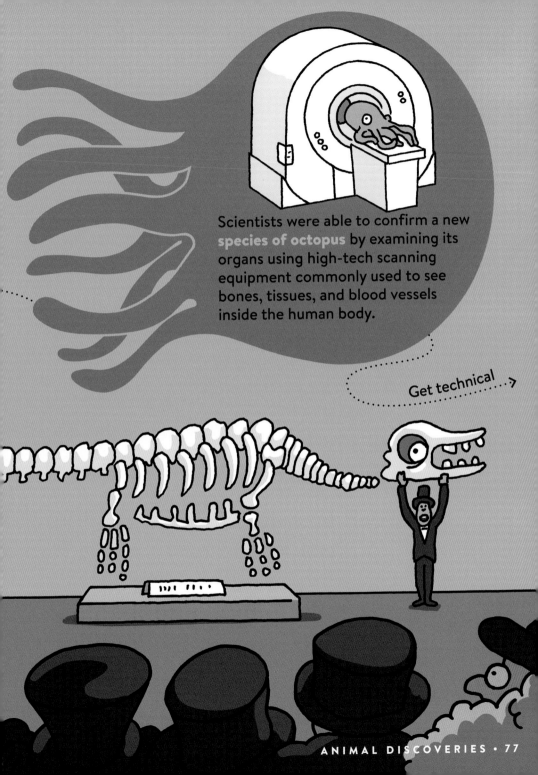

Scientists were able to confirm a new **species of octopus** by examining its organs using high-tech scanning equipment commonly used to see bones, tissues, and blood vessels inside the human body.

Get technical

Using satellite images to view Antarctica from space, scientists could see **emperor penguins' poop** on the ice—leading them to discover previously unknown colonies.

Researchers in Antarctica identified fossilized plant roots in scans of a sediment core, a sample of Earth's crust taken by drilling a cylindrical hole in the ground. The discovery revealed that Antarctica had **rainforests** 90 million years ago...

Getting warmer >

A squirrel's brain **gets bigger** in the fall, which may be because they're memorizing where they hide their nuts.

Because heat causes metal to expand, the Eiffel Tower **grows taller** in the summer.

Go to page 32

So brainy!

The bacteria in your gut can **change** with the seasons.

Under the microscope

Some bacteria can make ice.

Water-loving algae called *Ceratium* have **horns and armored plates**.

Tiny **"zombie" organisms** frozen for thousands of years under Arctic permafrost were brought back to life in the lab.

Some chalk is made from million-year-old microscopic skeletons of ocean-dwelling plankton

Voyage to the Red Planet

Scientists think microorganisms could one day be used to help mine for important metals on Mars

Similar to earthquakes on Earth,

MARSQUAKES

shake the surface of Mars.

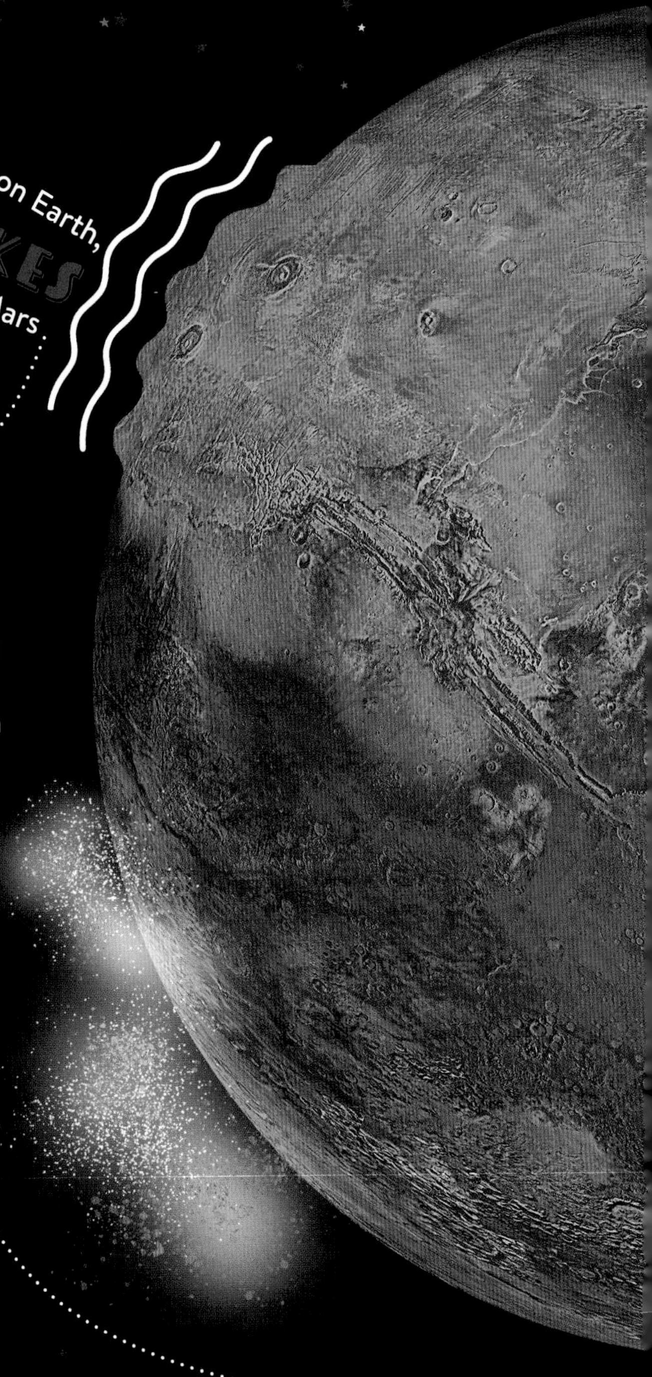

Mars sometimes has "mother of pearl" clouds that shimmer. They're made from frozen carbon dioxide—also known as dry ice.

Wild weather

Go to page 128

Astronauts are training to go to Mars by exploring Hawaiian lava tubes. Scientists think that when humans start visiting Mars, the planet's lava tubes may be the safest places to live...

Make it red hot!

K2-141b is a planet covered in lava seas and where it rains **rocks**.

The only **rock** that floats is called pumice, which is sometimes created by volcanoes. People once found a floating pumice **island** in the Pacific Ocean.

Scientists discovered a parrot-size **dinosaur** that had only one "finger" on each hand. They think it used the sole digit to dig for **insect** prey.

Paleontologists have found small stones in the **stomachs** of long-necked **dinosaurs**. They think the dinosaurs swallowed leaves whole and then swallowed the rocks to help grind up the leaves.

Assassin bugs are **insects** that have an unusual hunting method— they tap spiders with their antennae before they attack them. Researchers think that the tapping confuses and distracts the **spiders** and makes them less aggressive.

Island gigantism is a phenomenon where island-dwelling animals can become much larger than mainland species, as they have less competition for food. Galapagos **tortoises**, for example, can weigh more than 550 pounds (250kg).

Water is not digested like food—it's absorbed. Your **stomach** usually absorbs water in about 20 minutes or less.

Desert **tortoises** don't need to drink **water** for up to a year, because they store it in their bladders and absorb it during dry periods.

Male wolf **spiders** make purring **sounds** to attract partners. They do this by making the dried leaves they stand on vibrate.

Soundscape ecologists study **sounds** around the world. This helps them analyze how healthy a habitat is.

Get to work!

Fireworks designers use complex chemistry to create wow-worthy colors and shapes

Some dessert companies have professional **ice-cream scientists**

Scatologists study **animal poop** to learn about a critter's diet and the way it lives.

Feeling hungry?

Go to page 48

CHEWING GUM IS A FULL-TIME JOB FOR A GUMOLOGIST, WHO RESEARCHES AND TESTS GUM AND EVEN CREATES NEW FLAVORS.

Special zoologists called **snake milkers** extract venom from snake fangs to help medical researchers create lifesaving antivenom.

Slither onward →

The tails of some snakes, such as pit vipers and rattlesnakes,

GLOW BLUE

under ultraviolet light.

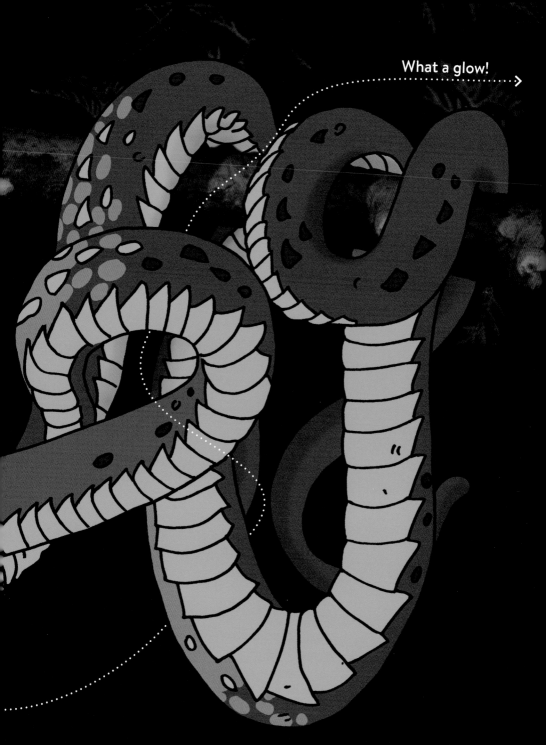

What a glow!

...Bioluminescence is the ability of organisms to create their own light. In the deep sea, the "**alarm jelly**" flashes blue light to warn off predators and attract or distract prey...

Gas particles colliding in Earth's atmosphere create the movement of the **northern lights**.

Zzzap! →

Light travels **100 times faster** than the electricity that powers the average house.

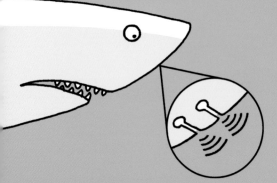

Sharks can sense electricity miles away through **jelly-filled tubes** on the surface of their skin, which helps them to locate their prey.

Go to page 34

There's a species of hornet that's **solar-powered:** Pigments in its tissues can trap light from the sun and turn it into electricity. How it uses the power is still a mystery.

Go green

To minimize litter, researchers are creating **drones** made from fungi. These drones are biodegradable, so they can be flown in places where they might crash and never be recovered

Engineers developed foldable solar panels inspired by

ORIGAMI

Fun with fungi!

Go to page 186

Waterless toilets use microbes to break down human waste and make fertilizer.

The world's tallest wind turbine, located in Germany, is 58 stories high

Power on

If every computer on Earth were to shut off for **one night**, the energy saved could power the Empire State Building for over **30 years**

....The **first known computer** was 50 feet (15m) long and weighed more thar

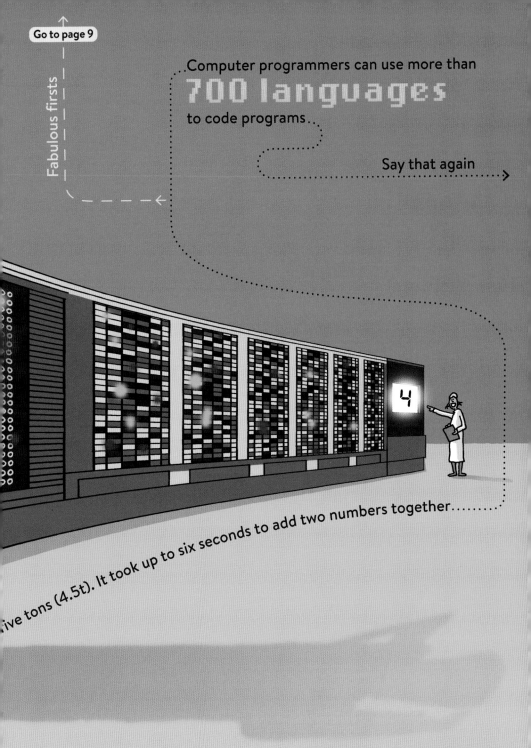

Go to page 9

Fabulous firsts

Computer programmers can use more than
700 languages
to code programs

Say that again

4

...ive tons (4.5t). It took up to six seconds to add two numbers together...

Speaking **multiple languages** can change the physical structure of your brain.

你好

Clouded leopards use their **tails** to balance as they climb through trees in their **rainforest** home.

Trees in the **rainforest** compete to grow tallest and reach the most **sunlight**.

The right side of a dog's brain tells the dog to wag its **tail** left, while the left side tells it to wag to the right.

The **heads** and limbs of prey decorate the nests of the "skull-collecting" **ant**.

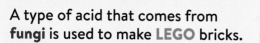

By testing DNA, researchers figured out **ants** were "farming" **fungi** 60 million years before humans learned to farm.

A type of acid that comes from **fungi** is used to make **LEGO** bricks.

A nuclear scientist at CERN used **LEGO** bricks to build a device on short notice, as the toy bricks can withstand powerful **radiation**.

The **radiation** from the sun has turned all the U.S. flags planted on the **moon** white.

In just one hour, **sunlight** provides our **planet** with more energy than humans use in the form of electricity in an entire year.

On the dwarf **planet** Pluto, there are mountains made of **ice**, but scientists aren't sure how they formed.

Mice have **teeth** that are harder than iron.

The **teeth** of a babirusa, a type of wild pig, grow so long they can grow outside of their mouths and back into their **heads**.

Balls of moss grow on the **ice** of some glaciers. Nicknamed "glacier **mice**," some are the size of tennis balls.

Though the **moon** may look perfectly round, its shape is closer to that of a **lemon**.

If you write a message with **lemon** juice and let it dry, it will become **invisible**. You can read the message if you heat the paper up a little.

Engineers are developing a technology to make cloaks that would turn the wearer **invisible**.

Engineer it!

The steel-and-glass Bailong Elevator, built into the side of a cliff in China, is the world's **tallest outdoor elevator**.

Engineers are working on a **solar-powered rocket** that could be three times more efficient than current rocket engines.

Up and away!

People in ancient China invented one of the **earliest rockets** made from a bamboo tube filled with gunpowder.

There's a spot in the Pacific Ocean nicknamed the "**spacecraft cemetery**." Old rockets, satellites, and even space stations are intentionally crashed here because it is the farthest place in the ocean from land.

To help people stranded on board sinking ships, rescuers on the coast of Tynemouth, U.K., fired rockets with an attached line, buoy, and pair of pants—people would **climb into the pants** to be pulled ashore.

Incredible artifacts

A German archaeologist discovered an ancient monument in Turkey that was built over 6,000 years before Stonehenge, U.K., featuring **huge stone pillars** carved with animals, including lions and scorpions. The purpose of the monument is still a mystery.

How mysterious

Some researchers think that a **parallel universe** may exist beyond our galaxy.

Some researchers think that a parallel universe may exist beyond our galaxy

Go to page 74 ↑

Explore the universe

No one knows why the ancient monument of Stonehenge was built, nor how the stones got there, but some studies suggest that they are arranged to amplify sound...

Many people, including scientists, have hunted for and reported sightings of a **hairy, humanlike creature**—named Bigfoot—roaming through forests. But no one knows for sure whether it exists...

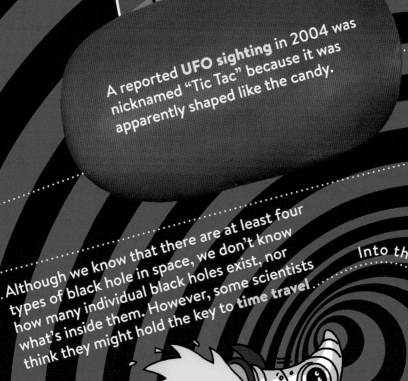

A reported **UFO sighting** in 2004 was nicknamed "Tic Tac" because it was apparently shaped like the candy.

Although we know that there are at least four types of black hole in space, we don't know how many individual black holes exist, nor what's inside them. However, some scientists think they might hold the key to **time travel**...

Into the hole

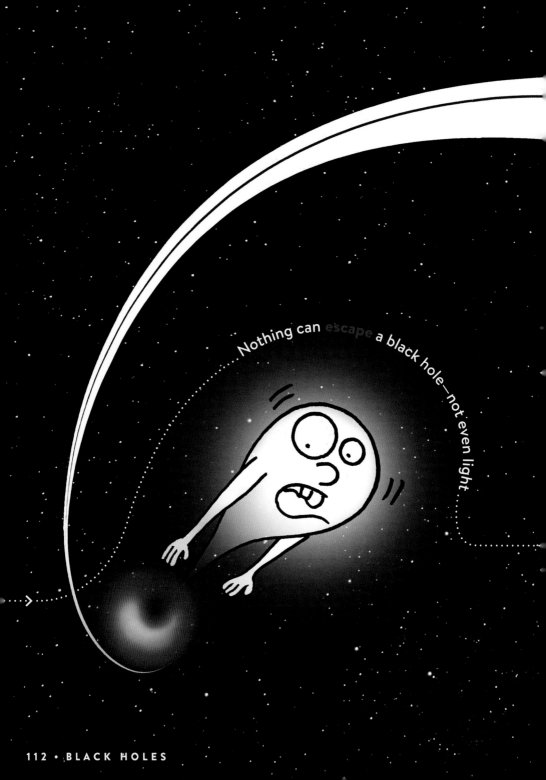

Nothing can *escape* a black hole—not even light

Spaghettification, also called
the noodle effect, happens
when an object is pulled toward
a black hole, stretching it out
like a piece of long, skinny pasta

Black holes can be pink because the gas surrounding them gives off pink light

How colorful

Some people have **synesthesia**, where the senses get mixed up in the brain so that they might smell color or see sound ....

Watermelon snow, caused by algae, can be pink or green, and it often has a sweet scent

It's snowing!

Go to page 84

Mission to Mars

There are snowstorms on Mars

In winter, collared lemmings grow large shovellike claws to dig through snow.

Some animals build their **dens** in snow. The snow traps air to keep animals warm, helping them survive.

Live it up!

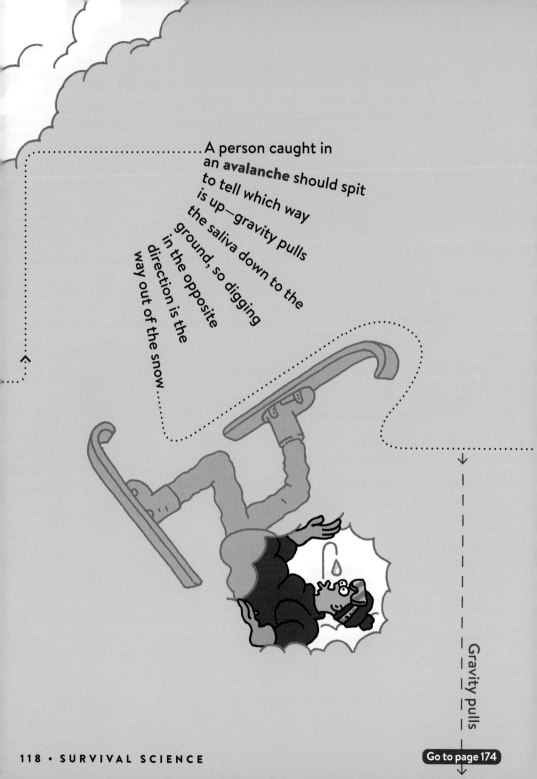

A person caught in an **avalanche** should spit to tell which way is up—gravity pulls the saliva down to the ground, so digging in the opposite direction is the way out of the snow

Gravity pulls

Go to page 174

One spacecraft carrying tardigrades—animals that can survive extreme temperatures and dehydration—**crash-landed** on to the moon. Scientists think these microscopic creatures survived...

If a bird eats a **stick insect**, the hard-shelled eggs inside the insect can still survive the bird's digestive system and hatch after they've been pooped out...

Eggs-actly!

Cassowaries—large birds
related to emus—lay
green eggs

Go to page 114

Cool colors

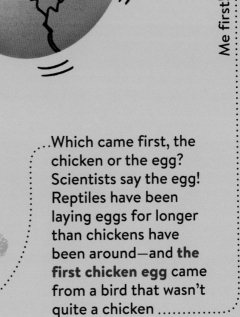

Me first!

..Which came first, the chicken or the egg? Scientists say the egg! Reptiles have been laying eggs for longer than chickens have been around—and **the first chicken egg** came from a bird that wasn't quite a chicken ....

Viruses were first studied in plants, not people, in the 1800s.

Some insects can spread **viruses** as they travel from plant to plant feeding on **nectar**.

Alarm **calls** from a prairie dog—a mammal that lives on the North American **grasslands**—tell other prairie dogs the size, color, and even type of nearby predators.

Mates for life, a pair of macaroni **penguins** recognize each other by their **calls**. They bow and wave their heads when they reunite.

On dry and open **grasslands**, **fires** can spread at speeds of 600 feet (183m) a minute.

Many plants produce **nectar** that contains caffeine. Scientists discovered that the caffeine improves memory in **honeybees**, helping them remember a plant's location.

Honeybees collect and carry pollen in basket-shaped structures on their **legs**.

The **legs** of a **penguin** look short, but that's because their feathers cover them to below the knee.

Africa has more **fires** each year than any other **continent**.

Traces of a lost **continent** dating from 150 million years ago were identified in some rock found in Canada.

More massive finds

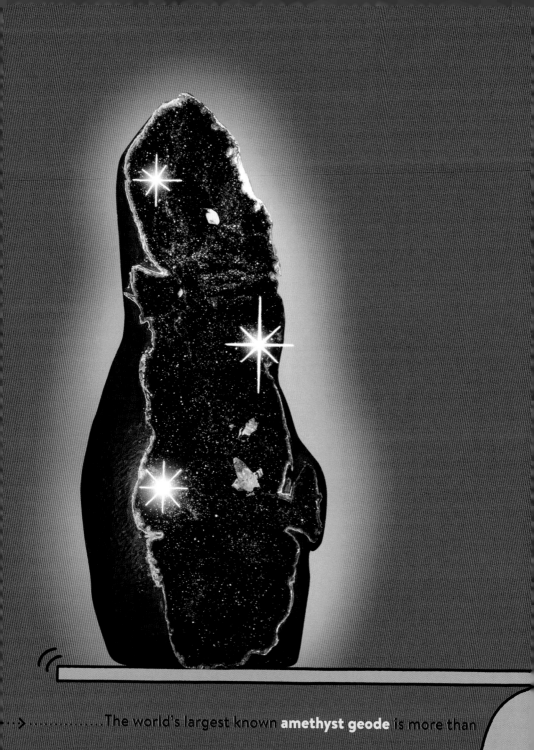

···>················ The world's largest known **amethyst geode** is more than

The Eye of the Sahara is a circular rock formation that looks like a **bull's-eye** and can be seen from space

All Olympic **curling stones** are made from a rare type of granite that is found only on Ailsa Craig, a tiny island off the west coast of Scotland.

The limestone rock at the top of **Mount Everest** was once at the bottom of the ocean. The rock contains the remains of invertebrates that lived underwater millions of years ago

Watch the forecast >

The Rock of Gibraltar is a huge **limestone rock** that dates back to the Jurassic era. It is home to Europe's only group of wild monkeys, which were once protected by the British army

Scientists can study stalagmites in caves to learn what weather was like in the past

Weather balloons

—used to collect weather data—get bigger as they go higher in the sky, sometimes inflating to become about as long as a school bus!

High in Earth's atmosphere, a rare kind of lightning called a red sprite looks like a **jellyfish's tentacles** stretching down from the sky

Tornado winds can reach speeds greater than the speeds of Formula One race cars

Charged **particles on the sun** can create weather in space. Sometimes these particles erupt from the sun's surface and can even cause power outages on Earth!

Sun's out

It's possible to work out the air temperature by counting a **cricket's chirps**, which get faster as the temperature rises

The sun is so big that more than a million

EARTHS

could fit inside it.

..Monarch
butterflies have
light-sensitive
antennae that help
them to navigate
using the position
of the sun...........

During a
total solar eclipse,
birds often stop tweeting—
the momentary darkness as
the moon blocks the sun's
light jump-starts
their nighttime
behavior.

To the moon!

Every year, the moon moves about 1½ inches (3.8cm) farther away from Earth

Keep moving

Go to page 20

There's a cloud around the moon—
it's made up of moon dust that's been
disturbed as meteorites have crashed
into the moon's surface

...NASA scientists have suggested that humans could one day live in **floating cities** built above the clouds on Venus...

Unlike other clouds, which are mostly made of liquid water droplets, cirrus clouds are made of **ice crystals**...................

A cumulus cloud can weigh as much as

100
elephants.

Flat, pancake-shaped **anvil clouds** form during thunderstorms.

Water, water, everywhere! ·····>

Scientists can actually make it rain. Called cloud seeding, the process involves sending objects such as drones into the clouds to **zap them** with electricity, which causes it to rain.

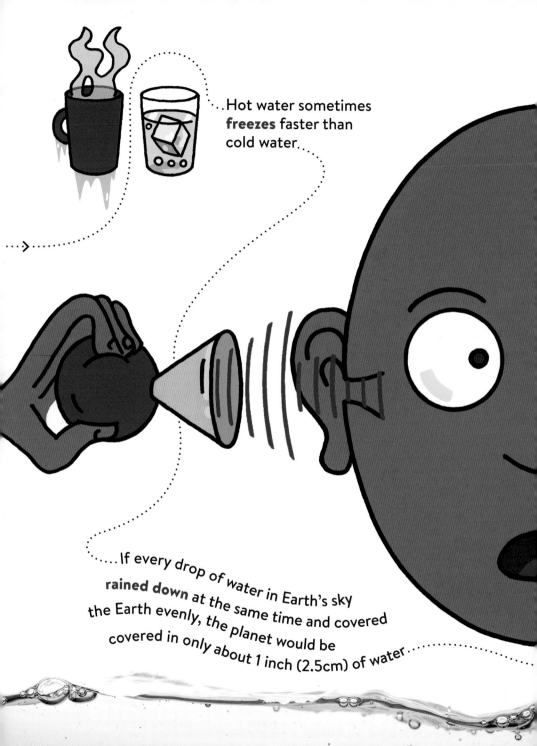

Hot water sometimes **freezes** faster than cold water.

If every drop of water in Earth's sky **rained down** at the same time and covered the Earth evenly, the planet would be covered in only about 1 inch (2.5cm) of water.

Hear that?

You hear **sounds traveling through water** as louder than sounds traveling through air. That's because when your head is underwater, sound waves vibrate your skull as well as your ear drums

Bats, whales, and dolphins send out sound waves that bounce back to them from nearby objects to help them navigate ...

Which way home?

Some violins are made with wood treated with fungi to create unique sounds ....

The first compasses, invented in China around 200 BCE, were made of **magnetic stone** and shaped like spoons— the handle of the spoon pointed south.

Scientists think that the ancient Egyptians were the first to use homing pigeons to **carry messages**. The pigeons can find their way back to their roost from thousands of miles away.

Early sailors in the northern hemisphere navigated their way across the sea by looking at the night sky to find Polaris, **the North Star**, which sits above the North Pole

Twinkle, twinkle

Australia is **moving north** by about 2.7 inches (7cm) each year. In 2017, Australian officials relocated the country's GPS coordinates by 5.9 feet (1.8m)

Arctic foxes have **white** fur in the winter to blend in with **snow** and darker fur in the summer.

Algae that grows on **snow** supports life inside glaciers. Ice **worms** venture up to the surface of glaciers to eat the algae twice a day.

Individual stars can be different colors, including blue, yellow, orange, red, and **white**. Their color is caused by their temperature.

Helium has an extremely low **boiling** point of minus 452.1 degrees Fahrenheit (-268.9°C).

The **rain** on Jupiter is made of **helium**— the element we use in gas form to fill party balloons.

Known as 'the **Boiling** River', a stretch of water in the **Amazon rainforest** can reach temperatures of up to 200 degrees Fahrenheit (93°C)— or very near boiling point.

The **Amazon rainforest** is home to millions of **ants**—collectively they weigh more than all the monkeys that live there.

Scientists once discovered a new species of **ant** in a frog's **vomit**.

Worms hear using special cells in their skin that detect **sound**.

It's impossible for **sound** to travel through empty space because there is no **air**.

All animals need **air** to breathe, but some **cockroaches** can survive underwater for up to 30 minutes.

Scientists have fed **cockroaches dust** from the moon's surface.

There's a little bit of **dust** in every drop of **rain**.

Hurling their stomachs outside of their bodies like **vomit** is a way that some **fish**, such as sharks, clean them.

The genetic code that forms your limbs and lungs originates from a 50-million-year-old **fish**—and is still present in all human beings today.

It's in the genes

Some **octopuses** can edit their own genes
to adapt to their surroundings.

People with a gene called ADRB1 need less sleep than people without this gene

Catch some zzz ⟶

All people with the gene for **blue eyes** can be traced back to a common ancestor

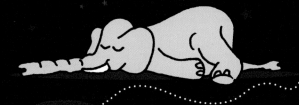

Wild elephants sleep for just **two hours each day**— that's less time than any other mammal

Rabbits can sleep with their **eyes open**

Roughly 15 percent of all kids **sleepwalk**

According to NASA scientists, the **perfect nap** is 10 to 20 minutes long

Game on!

People who play video games are more likely to experience **lucid dreaming**, the ability to control your dreams

...The first **video games** were invented in

science
laboratories

Go to page 58

More experiments

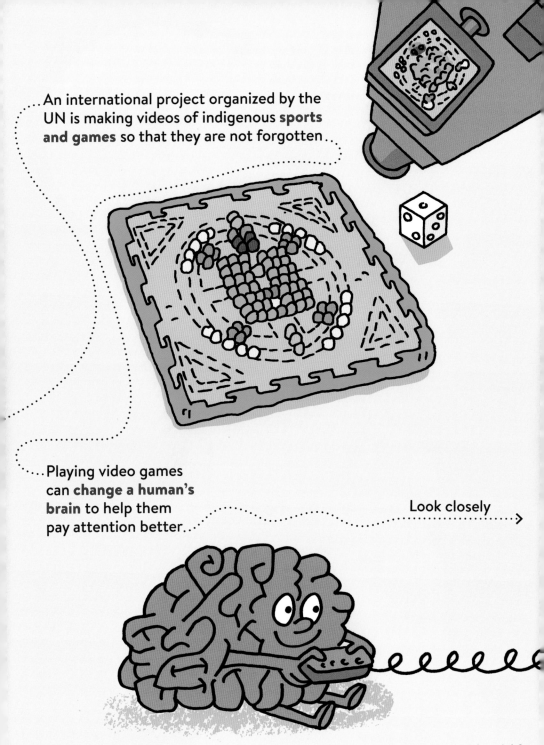

An international project organized by the UN is making videos of indigenous **sports and games** so that they are not forgotten.

Playing video games can **change a human's brain** to help them pay attention better.

Look closely ⟶

The California **purple sea urchin** has light-detecting cells all over its surface, so that its entire body functions like an eye.

Chameleons have close to 360-degree vision and can move each eye by itself.

Most humans can see more **shades of green** than of any other color.

A camera that mimics **how sharks see** revealed they glow to each other in the darkness of the ocean....

Owls can't move their eyes, so they **swivel their heads** to see in different directions

More clever inventions

The world's **smallest rideable motorcycle** is as tall as a soda can is wide. Its Swedish inventor named it Smalltoe, and he rode on it for 33 feet (10m).

A tech company has created a **doggy door** that owners can control remotely, or the dog can open and close from a chip in its collar. Even when the owner is out, live video and two-way audio keep human and furry friends in touch.

Visayan warty pigs use pieces of

BARK

to dig holes in the ground to make their nests

Digger wasps seal the tunnels to their nests, using pebbles to press down the soil at its entrance

"Firehawk" raptors in Australia carry burning branches as they fly, spreading wildfires on purpose to snatch prey fleeing from the flames.

Into the flames →

People in ancient China were among the first to start fires using sunlight reflected off a **mirror**.

Mount Wingen in Australia, also known as "**Burning Mountain**," has a fire around 100 feet (30m) below its surface that has been burning for more than 6,000 years.

Pistachios have natural oils inside them that can heat up, causing the nuts to **burst into flames**.

Strike that >

Wildfires

can create clouds that have their own lightning.......

Forest
fires travel

faster uphill

than they do
downhill because heat
rises, so trees or grass above the
fire will heat up and burn more quickly.

Helicopters flying through storms can cause

LIGHTNING

A bolt of lightning can be 400 miles (644km) long—that's about four times as big as Belgium is wide

Lightning provides vital elements such as **nitrogen** to the soil, which keeps grass and other plants healthy.

Dig in the dirt

In Hawaii, tea is grown in **volcanic** soil

Night crawler earthworms leave plugs on the top of their burrows—the plugs are usually made of dirt and minerals they've **pooped out**

More eruptions

Go to page 192

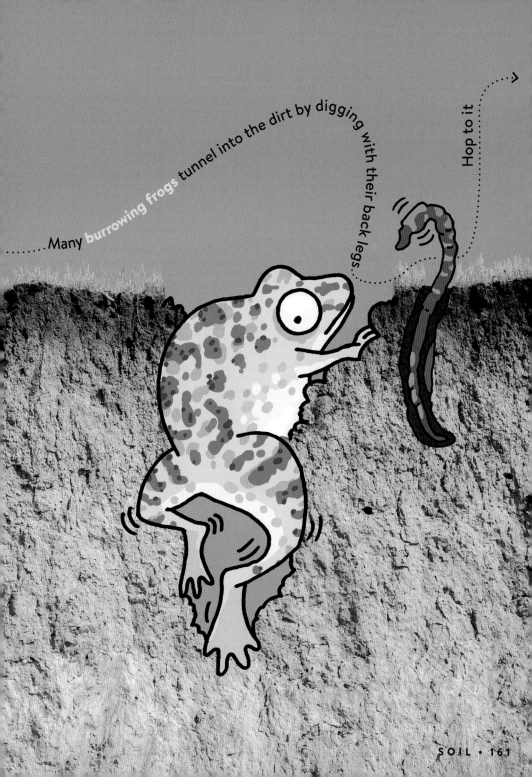

Many **burrowing frogs** tunnel into the dirt by digging with their back legs.

Hop to it

On the Southeast Asian island of Borneo, scientists discovered a frog with no **lungs**.

An energy company built a 16-foot-tall (5m) pair of **lungs** that filled with colorful gases to represent dangerous air pollution in **London**.

On the **day** they're born, giraffes take their first **steps**.

You would have to take about 50 million **steps** to walk the full length of Earth's **equator**.

Before our solar system had planets, the sun's **equator** was surrounded by only a swirling disc of **gas** and dust. The planets formed out of this disc.

People in London can tell time using Big Ben, a massive clock that engineers keep accurate by placing pennies inside its mechanism.

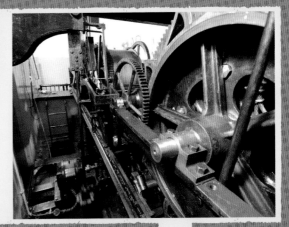

Ancient Egyptians made early forms of clocks using stones that cast shadows.

Your shadow at any specific time of day is longer in the winter than it is in the summer.

Jellyfish venom could one day be used to treat illnesses such as cancer.

Get well soon

Some galaxies have a stream of gas that looks like a long tentacle—scientists call these "jellyfish galaxies."

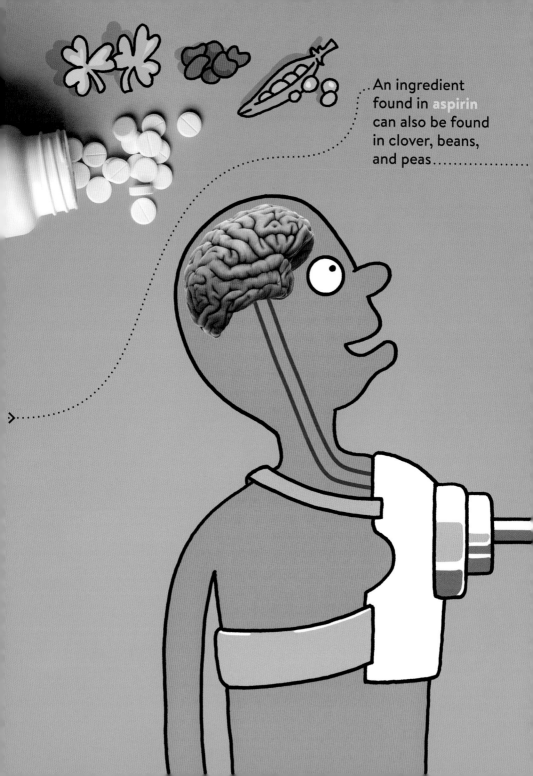

An ingredient found in **aspirin** can also be found in clover, beans, and peas.................

Researchers created BirdNET, an artificial intelligence that helps identify different species of birds from their songs alone.

Spread your wings

Using 3D printers, scientists have created **new beaks** for injured toucans.

The fossil of an ancient bird discovered in Antarctica had a **wingspan** wider than the height of a two-story building.

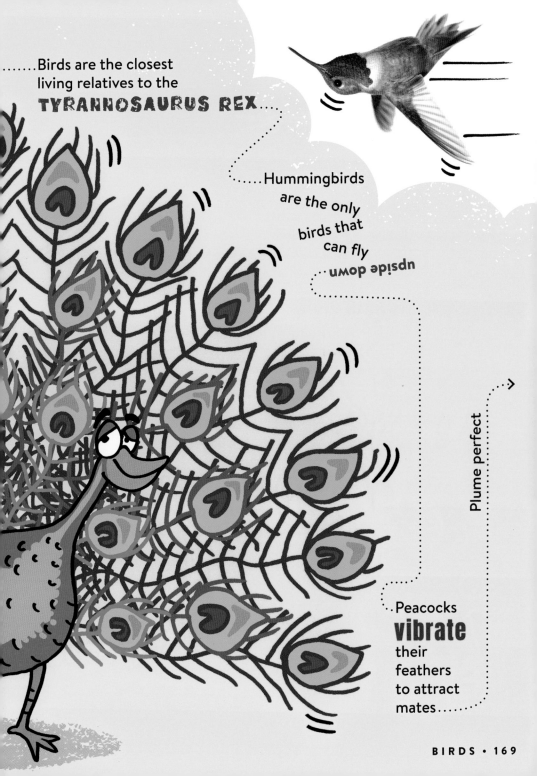

......Birds are the closest living relatives to the **TYRANNOSAURUS REX**......

......Hummingbirds are the only birds that can fly upside down

Plume perfect

Peacocks **vibrate** their feathers to attract mates......

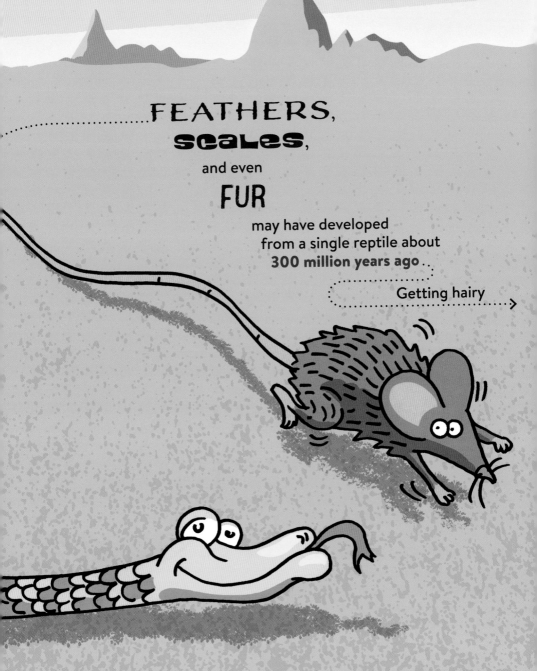

FEATHERS, **SCALES,** and even **FUR** may have developed from a single reptile about **300 million years ago**

Getting hairy →

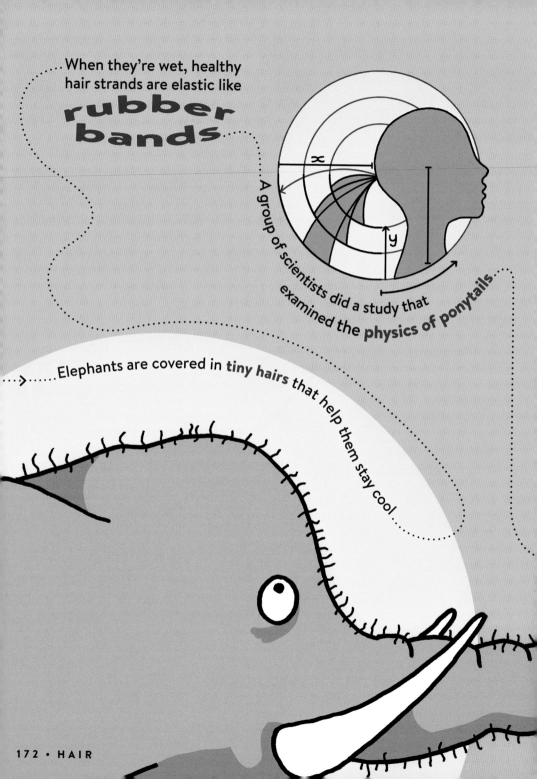

When they're wet, healthy hair strands are elastic like

rubber bands

A group of scientists did a study that examined the **physics of ponytails**

Elephants are covered in **tiny hairs** that help them stay cool

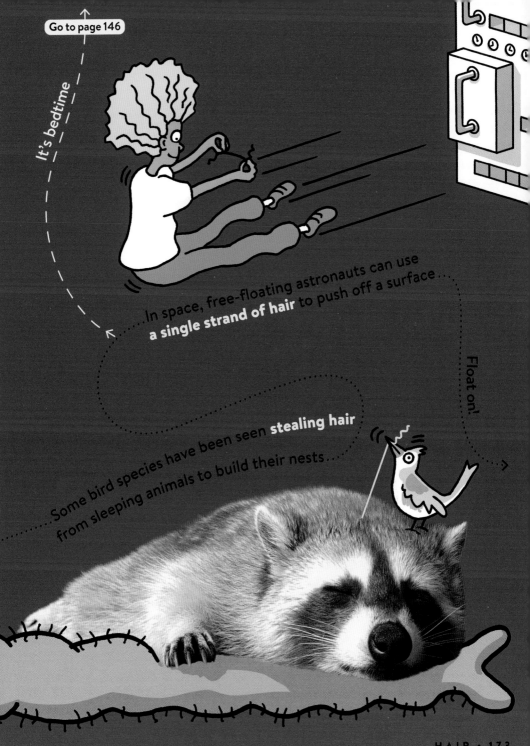

Go to page 146

It's bedtime

In space, free-floating astronauts can use **a single strand of hair** to push off a surface...

Some bird species have been seen **stealing hair** from sleeping animals to build their nests...

Float on!

In the Hudson Bay area of Canada, people **weigh a little bit less**, because Hudson Bay has less gravity than any other known spot on Earth...

An experiment on **twin astronauts**, one on Earth and the other in space, helped us to understand how gravity affects the human body...

Go to page 44

Amazing anatomy

...On Earth our muscles help support the weight of our bodies, but in space astronauts are almost weightless, so their muscles don't need to work as hard. To keep their muscles strong, astronauts need to exercise for about two hours every day......

As the dinosaur *Limusaurus inextricabilis* grew up, its teeth fell out. Instead of getting new **teeth** as adults, the dinosaurs grew **beaks**.

Tapping **beaks** together is how shoebill storks—named for their beaks, which are shaped like **shoes**—greet each other.

The strongest muscle in your body is in your jaw. Using all your jaw muscles together, your **teeth** can crush down on food with a force that rivals the weight of a refrigerator!

Chemists say some of the smelliest **odors** on Earth come from molecules in a skunk's spray, which contains the same kinds of molecules found in rotting meat and bad **breath**.

The Dragon's **Breath** chili pepper, one of the hottest peppers in the world, was cultivated as a natural medicine to numb **skin** before surgery.

A navel stone is a hard ball formed by dead **skin**, dirt, and oil inside your **belly button**.

Using microbes that grow on **belly buttons** and other parts of the skin, a researcher and an artist teamed up to create a new kind of **cheese**.

One **shoe** company is sending the materials it uses to make soles into space. It hopes that by studying how these materials react in low **gravity**, it can make better footwear.

Reduced **gravity** means that some **bacteria** grow and mutate more quickly in space.

Almost all **fish** have a backbone, except for "snot eels," which look like slimy **socks**.

Bacteria in the mucus of some fish act like a slimy barrier to protect the **fish** from other microorganisms that could make them sick.

Sweaty **socks** have **odors** that attract mosquitoes.

Some explorers on long expeditions claimed they needed fresh **milk** for their health. In the 1930s one group took three cows to **Antarctica**.

The big freeze

Cheese might have been invented by accident, when people in ancient times stored **milk** in a pouch made from an animal's stomach.

The world's longest glacier was about 440 miles (708km) long when it was first discovered near **Antarctica** in the 1950s.

Glaciers store three-quarters of the fresh water on Earth.

Some glaciers look blue because the ice is so densely packed that it absorbs red and yellow light

Make a splash!

Go to page 136

Water from melting glaciers high up in the Himalayan mountains provides water for growing crops in the lowlands thousands of miles away

On the farm

Some butter is naturally yellow from the grass and

FLoWeRS

that cows eat

Some farms have **self-driving robots** that can measure the height of plants, estimate how much crop is growing, and even tell how healthy a field is...

Beep boop!

Archaeologists used a **HUMANOID ROBOT** diver to recover artifacts from a sunken shipwreck

Dive in

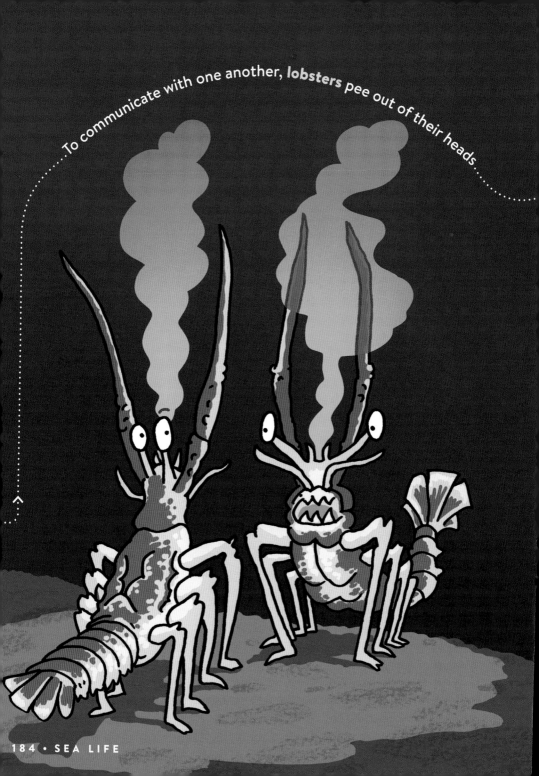

To communicate with one another, *lobsters* pee out of their heads

The manatee, also called a sea cow, swims so **s l o w l y** near the water's surface that algae grow on its back.

Seahorses do not have stomachs or teeth...

A **mushroom-shaped creature**, once thought to be a new species, is actually part of a jellyfish that detaches when the animal is disturbed........

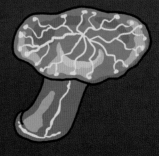

Terrific teeth!

Go to page 18

Fun with fungus

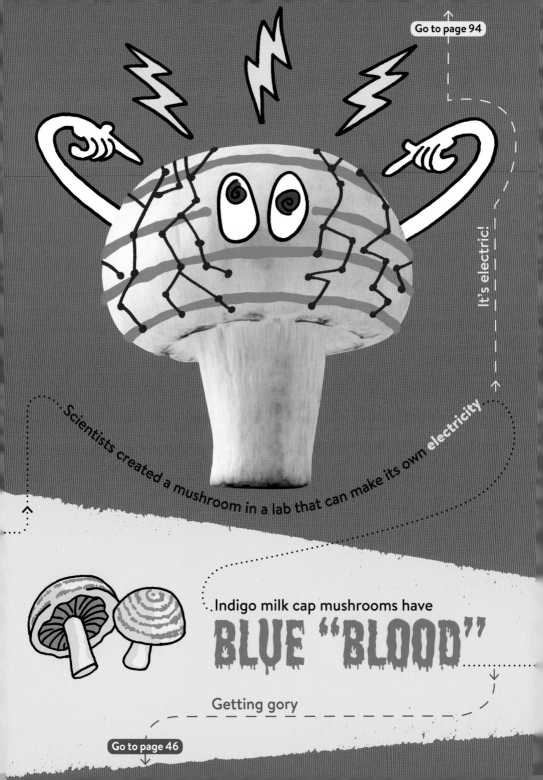

Go to page 94

It's electric!

Scientists created a mushroom in a lab that can make its own electricity

Indigo milk cap mushrooms have

BLUE "BLOOD"

Getting gory

Go to page 46

Many fungi **anchor themselves** to tree roots to get their nutrients. In return, the fungi expand the trees' root systems, allowing the trees to soak up even more goodness from the soil

Scientists have discovered a fungus that can **break down plastic** in just a few weeks. On its own, plastic can take up to 1,000 years to decompose

Find your bestie >

Fungi can turn plants into **ethanol**, a fuel that can be used to power some cars

Colombian lesserblack tarantulas and dotted humming frogs **share a burrow**—the tarantulas protect the frogs from predators, and the frogs munch on the ants that try to eat the tarantula eggs.

Mongooses snack on the pesky ticks on warthogs' backs—so they help each other, much like Timon and Pumbaa's **special bond** in Disney's *The Lion King*...

Animal aid

One type of moth creates an ultrasonic **click** sound that scares away **bats**.

The **knees** of some reindeer **click** when they walk. The sound helps the herd stay together in snowstorms.

Warthogs have cushioned **knees** so they can kneel while they graze.

Each human **foot** has about 125,000 **sweat** glands.

Scientists can study Earth's changing climate by examining ancient **bat** **poop**.

Up to 80 percent of your **poop** is **bacteria**— much of it alive.

Bacteria are no match for slug slime, which not only helps the creature move, but also protects it against infection.

Slugs have bodies that act like one slimy, muscular **foot** to pull them along surfaces.

Volcanoes sometimes **smell** of rotten eggs. The odor comes from sulfur gas in the ground.

The bacteria on your skin gives sweat its **smell**.

Cause an eruption

Iceland is powered by volcanic activity. Most people in the country heat their homes with **geothermal power**, which is harnessed from heat and steam from magma.......

Rapidly cooling lava turns into obsidian, a rock that has edges **sharper than steel**. Some surgeons use it as a blade when performing operations.

↑
Go to page 96

Go green!

↑ There are volcanoes under the ocean. The **deepest eruption** ever discovered is nearly 3 miles (4.8km) below the water's surface.

Smog that comes from a volcano is called

vog

—it can eat away at objects just like battery acid does.

More minerals >

Researchers discovered a new type of **blue mineral**, named petrovite, on top of a Russian volcano.

Rubies and sapphires

may be different colors, but they're made from the same mineral, called corundum.

Alexandrite **changes color** in different kinds of light—it can turn green in daylight and red under candlelight

Some studies suggest that if they weighed the same, a **cricket** would contain more of the mineral iron than a steak

Creepy crawly

When threatened, a click beetle uses a part of its body to **do a flip**, which makes a loud clicking noise.

> Some cicadas spend **17 years underground** before they hatch from their eggs and millions of the creatures emerge together.

Go to page 88

Cool careers

Researchers are designing **bee-size drones** to help pollinate plants.

What's next?

In the hot afternoon sun, dung beetles stand on **dung balls** to keep their feet cool.

Forensic entomologists study bugs to help **solve crimes**.

Companies are developing technology that could collect data about your body to create a

"DIGITAL TWIN"

—a virtual version of you that doctors could use to track your health.

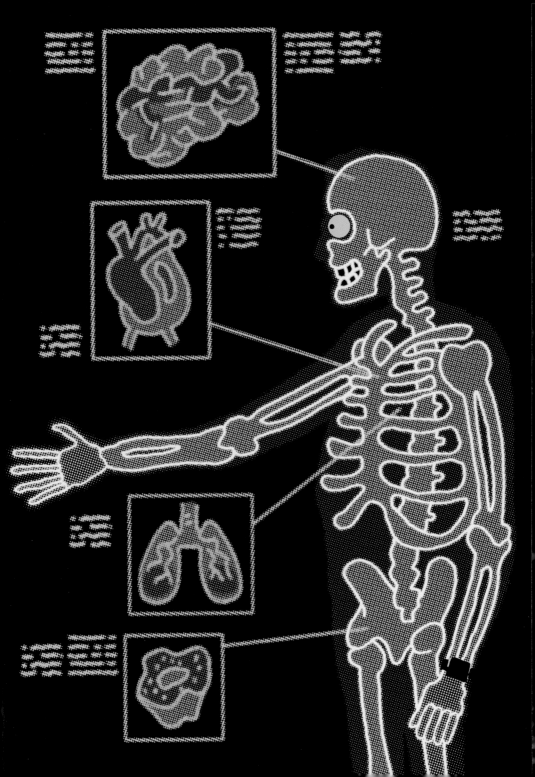

Sound Like a Scientist Quiz

On your journey through Science FACTopia, you have discovered lots of different things that scientists can study—from volcanoes to video games! Areas of scientific study often have technical names—for example, the study of hair is called trichology. Can you match these subjects with their scientific names?

1. Odontology (chomp chomp)...............................
2. Horology (tick tock)
3. Ichthyology (just keep swimming)
4. Hematology (hope you're not squeamish)
5. Gemology (ooh sparkly!)
6. Toxicology (CAUTION)
7. Phenology (change is in the air)
8. Oology (what's for breakfast?)
9. Meteorology (check the forecast)
10. Heliology (shine bright)
11. Hydrology (glug glug)
12. Somnology (catch some zz's)
13. Ludology (let's play)
14. Pyrology (it's getting hot in here)
15. Ornithology (tweet tweet)
16. Plumology (as light as a...)
17. Glaciology (slooowly does it)
18. Mycology (fun with...)
19. Volcanology (you got this one!)
20. Entomology (buzz buzz)

a. Fish
b. Eggs
c. Teeth
d. Feathers
e. Games
f. Fire
g. Birds
h. Sleep
i. Weather
j. Seasons
k. Glaciers
l. Fungi
m. Insects
n. Gemstones
o. Volcanoes
p. Blood
q. Time
r. Poisons
s. The sun
t. Water

Answers on p.205

Index

L

laboratories 57, 58–9, 148
lakes 68
languages 99, 100–1
lava tubes 85
LEGO 102
lemon juice 103
LENS-X wind tunnel 58
life spans 54
light 38, 90, 92–3, 102, 103, 112–13, 156, 178
lightning 17, 73, 128, 157, 158–9
limestone rock 127
Limusaurus inextricabilis 176
lobsters 184
London 162, 163
Lucy 11
lungs 142, 162

m

manatees 185
manta ray 24
marine artifacts 68, 182
Mars 41, 83, 84–5, 116
math 30
metals 61, 83
meteors/meteorites 30, 40, 133
methane 39
mica 61
mice 103
microbes 97, 176
microorganisms 82–3, 177
milk 177
Milky Way 28, 29, 71
minerals 50, 61, 160, 193, 194–5
Monarch butterflies 130
mongooses 189
monkeys 66, 127, 142
monuments 108, 110
moon 6, 27, 28, 41, 56, 72, 73, 102–3, 119, 131, 132–3, 143
moon trees 6, 73
mosquitoes 177
moss 16, 103
moths 190
motion 20–1

motorcycles 22, 152
Mount Everest 59, 127
Mount Wingen 156
mud 38
mud pots 38
mummies, Egyptian 18, 31
muscles 175, 176
mushrooms 186–7
music 14–15, 166
mysteries, science 110–11

n

naked mole rats 19
nanotechnology 166
NASA 134, 147
navel stones 176
navigation 130, 139, 140–1
nectar 122, 123
nests 72, 102, 154, 173
neutron stars 60
nitrogen 159
noodle effect 113
northern lights 93
nuclear pasta 60

o

oak trees 17
obsidian 192
oceans 68–9, 72
octopuses 25, 77, 144
orchids 73
origami 96
ostriches 24
owls 151
oxygen 25

p

Pacific Ocean 86, 106
paleontologists 11, 76, 86
parallel universes 110
parrots 10
peacocks 169
peanut butter 49
pee 44, 184
penguins 78, 122, 123
periodic table 64
petrovite 193
physics 56–7

pigeons 72, 140
pigs 12, 38, 154
pistachios 156
planets 24, 162
plankton 83
plants 14–17, 79, 187, 197
plastic 61, 187
Pluto 103
poisons 66–7
polar bears 117, 125
Polaris 141
ponytails 172
poop 6, 59, 78, 88, 97, 119, 160, 191
potatoes 60
prairie dogs 122
pumice 86
pumpkins 48
pyrite 60

R

rabbits 146
radiation 102
radium 64
rain 135, 136, 142, 143
rainforests 79, 102, 142
red sprite 128
reindeer 38, 190
reptiles 76, 121, 171
rescues 107
research technology 78–9
rivers 68
robots 21, 181, 182–3
Rock of Gibraltar 127
rock nettle 17
rockets 104, 106–7
rocks 40–1, 86, 126–7
Romans 38
rubies 194

S

S2 29
sailors 141
salt 62
sand 38, 61
sandbox tree 7, 39
sapphires 50, 194
satellite images 78
Saturn 24

Meet the FACTopians

Rose Davidson is an author, editor, and researcher based in Cincinnati, Ohio. She likes writing about wacky animal behaviors, awesome stuff in space, and other cool science stories. Rose studied anthropology in college, where she put on her science hat to learn about the world's many cultures, languages, and primates. Her favorite fact in this book is that peanut butter can be turned into diamonds.

Andy Smith is an award-winning illustrator. A graduate of the Royal College of Art, London, U.K., he creates artwork that has an optimistic, handmade feel. Creating the illustrations for *Science FACTopia!* brought even more surprises, from dancing plants to exploding pistachio nuts! Andy's favorite fact to draw was the romantic peacock shaking his feathers. When he discovered the fact about machines creating art he was very worried he wouldn't be needed anymore, but Lawrence the designer told him he was better than any machine.

Lawrence Morton is an art director and designer based in London, U.K. His greatest scientific achievement to date is to create an alarm for use when running a bath: It sounds when the water is reaching a dangerous level. His favorite fact was about machines creating art—don't tell Andy but he was quite excited by this possibility!

Sources

Scientists and other experts are discovering new facts and updating information all the time. That's why our FACTopia team has checked that every fact that appears in this book is based on multiple trustworthy sources and has been verified by the Britannica team. Of the hundreds of sources used in this book, here is a list of key websites we consulted.

News Organizations
abcnews.go.com
theatlantic.com
bbc.com
bbc.co.uk
cbc.ca
cbsnews.com
cnet.com
cnn.com
cntraveler.com
theguardian.com
kids.nationalgeographic.
   com
nationalgeographic.com
nationalgeographic.org
nbcnews.com
npr.org
nytimes.com
reuters.com
sci-news.com
sciencefocus.com
scientificamerican.com
slate.com
smh.com.au
time.com
washingtonpost.com
wired.com
usatoday.com
vice.com
vox.com

Government, Scientific, and Academic Organizations
asc-csa.gc.ca
audubon.org
britannica.com
clevelandclinic.org
energy.gov
gia.edu
geology.utah.gov
issnationallab.org
jstor.org
loc.gov

merriam-webster.com
nature.com
nasa.gov
ncbi.nlm.nih.gov
noaa.gov
nps.gov
royalsocietypublishing.org
sciencedirect.com
sciencemag.org
usda.gov
usgs.gov

Museums and Zoos
amnh.org
animals.sandiegozoo.org
carnegiemuseums.org
museum.wa.gov.au
national-aquarium.co.uk
nationalzoo.si.edu
nhm.ac.uk
ocean.si.edu
si.edu
smithsonianmag.com
torontozoo.com

Universities
animaldiversity.org
cornell.edu
harvard.edu
hawaii.edu
illinois.edu
news.mit.edu
oregonstate.edu
osu.edu
stanford.edu
stanforddaily.com
ucsd.edu
umich.edu
washington.edu
yale.edu

Other Websites
atlasobscura.com
awf.org
discovermagazine.com
gemsociety.org
geology.com
guinnessworldrecords.com
inaturalist.org
livescience.com
mentalfloss.com
newscientist.com
nwf.org
oceanconservancy.org
pbs.org
phys.org
popsci.com
popularmechanics.com
science.org
sciencedaily.com
space.com
theverge.com
unep.org
wcs.org
wwf.org.au

Picture Credits

The publisher would like to thank the following for permission to reproduce their photographs and illustrations. While every effort has been made to credit images, the publisher apologizes for any errors or omissions and will be pleased to make any necessary corrections in future editions of the book.

**BRITANNICA
BOOKS**

Britannica Books is an imprint of What on Earth Publishing,
published in collaboration with Britannica, Inc.
The Black Barn, Wickhurst Farm, Tonbridge, Kent, TN11 8PS, United Kingdom
30 Ridge Road Unit B, Greenbelt, Maryland, 20770, United States

First published in the United States in 2024

Written by Rose Davidson
Illustrated by Andy Smith
Designed by Lawrence Morton
Text developed by Wonderlab Group, LLC
Edited by Judy Barratt
Picture research by Susannah Jayes
Indexed by Vanessa Bird

Encyclopaedia Britannica
Alison Eldridge, Managing Editor; Michele Rita Metych, Fact-checking Supervisor

Britannica Books
Nancy Feresten, Publisher; Natalie Bellos, Editorial Director; Meg Osborne, Editor;
Andy Forshaw, Art Director; Alenka Oblak, Head of Production

Library of Congress Cataloging-in-Publication Data available upon request

ISBN: 9781804660256

1 3 5 7 9 10 8 6 4 2
Printed in China
DC/Foshan, China/09/2023

whatonearthbooks.com
britannica-books.com

Welcome to FACTopia, where each fact leads on to the next in endlessly entertaining ways!

FACTopia!
Follow the TRAIL of 400 FACTS

The rings on an adult mountain goat's horns tell you how old it is.

BY KATE HALE

Illustrated by ANDY SMITH

RETURN TO FACTopia!
Follow the TRAIL of MORE 400 FACTS

At night, giraffes quietly hum to one another.

BY KATE HALE

Illustrated by ANDY SMITH

GROSS FACTopia!
Follow the TRAIL of FOUL 400 FACTS

Hippopotamuses spin their tails while they poop.

BY PAIGE TOWLER

Illustrated by ANDY SMITH

ANIMAL FACTopia!
Follow the TRAIL of BEASTLY 400 FACTS

Chameleons change the colour of their skin to help them cool down.

BY JULIE BEER

Illustrated by ANDY SMITH

HISTORY FACTopia!
Follow ye olde TRAIL of 400 FACTS

The ancient Egyptians mummified snakes

BY PAIGE TOWLER

Illustrated by ANDY SMITH

SCIENCE FACTopia!
STEM-tastic
Follow the TRAIL of 400 FACTS

Lobsters pee out of their faces to communicate.

By ROSE DAVIDSON

Illustrated by ANDY SMITH

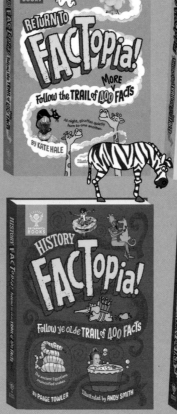

Enter the world of FACTopia here!